Ottawa Senators

Claryssa Lozano

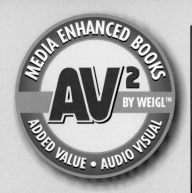

AV² provides enriched content that supplements and complements this book. Weigl's AV² books strive to create inspired learning and engage young minds in a total learning experience.

Your AV² Media Enhanced books come alive with...

Audio
Listen to sections of the book read aloud.

Key Words
Study vocabulary, and complete a matching word activity.

Video
Watch informative video clips.

Quizzes
Test your knowledge.

Embedded Weblinks
Gain additional information for research.

Slide Show
View images and captions, and prepare a presentation.

Try This!
Complete activities and hands-on experiments.

... and much, much more!

Go to **www.av2books.com**, and enter this book's unique code.

BOOK CODE

K 3 3 2 8 9 3

AV² by Weigl brings you media enhanced books that support active learning.

Published by AV² by Weigl
350 5th Avenue, 59th Floor
New York, NY 10118
Websites: www.av2books.com   www.weigl.com

Library of Congress Control Number: 2014951867

ISBN 978-1-4896-3167-1 (hardcover)
ISBN 978-1-4896-4017-8 (softcover)
ISBN 978-1-4896-3168-8 (single-user eBook)
ISBN 978-1-4896-3169-5 (multi-user eBook)

Printed in the United States of America in Brainerd, Minnesota
1 2 3 4 5 6 7 8 9 0 19 18 17 16 15

032015
WEP050315

Senior Editor Heather Kissock
Art Director Terry Paulhus

Photo Credits
Every reasonable effort has been made to trace ownership and to obtain permission to reprint copyright material. The publishers would be pleased to have any errors or omissions brought to their attention so that they may be corrected in subsequent printings.

Weigl acknowledges Getty Images and iStock as its primary image suppliers for this title.

Ottawa Senators

CONTENTS

Introduction

Nearly a century before Senator stars Alexei Yashin, Dany Heatley, or Erik Karlsson ever laced up a pair of skates, there was a hockey team playing in Ottawa. The original Ottawa Senators began play back in 1884, although they did not join the National Hockey League (NHL) until 1917. The Sens left the NHL in 1934, only to return 58 years later, in 1992. The Senators were lovable losers from 1992 through 1996, failing to reach the **playoffs**, or even 20 wins, in each season.

Goalie Ron Tugnutt made a total of 155 saves during the 1997 playoffs.

However, once coach Jacques Martin took over, the Sens began improving, making 11 straight playoff appearances from 1997 to 2008. The Senators won the Presidents' Trophy, awarded to the NHL team with the most points that year, in 2003. Still, their greatest achievement was in 2007, when they made it to the Stanley Cup Final, losing to the Anaheim Ducks in five games.

Ottawa
SENATORS

Arena Canadian Tire Centre

Division Atlantic

Head Coach Dave Cameron

Location Ottawa, Ontario, Canada

NHL Stanley Cup Titles None

Nicknames The Sens

Daniel Alfredsson had a career-high 103 points during the 2005–2006 season and was a big part of the 2007 Senators team that reached the Stanley Cup Final.

1
Stanley Cup Final Appearance

14
Playoff Appearances

4
Division Titles

1
Conference Championship

History

Alexei Yashin was the first player ever chosen by the Senators.

When the NHL version of the Senators came to Ottawa in 1992, a handful of the city's oldest residents recalled the original Senators, who had played in the NHL from 1917 until 1934. During those 17 seasons, the team captured five Stanley Cups, although the league was much smaller than today's version. The NHL had only four teams beginning in 1917, and nine teams by 1934. On December 6, 1990, the city of Ottawa was once again awarded an NHL **franchise**. Two years later, the Sens were skating onto the ice to play their first game against the Montreal Canadiens. They won that day 5-3, a promising start for the young team.

Despite suffering through a few lost seasons at the beginning, the team and its fans pressed on. The Sens began showing progress by the 1996 season with their first playoff appearance. Although they have not won a Stanley Cup during more than 20 NHL seasons in the modern era, they have had 14 playoff appearances. During the 2006–2007 season, the Sens made it to the Stanley Cup Final, losing to the Anaheim Ducks. With **All-Star** Erik Karlsson as their new captain, and a very strong defense, the team is working hard to bring the Cup back to Ottawa.

Cyril Leeder led the "Bring back the Senators" campaign in 1989–1990, and is credited with bringing the Sens back to Ottawa. He is currently the team president.

The Arena

The Canadian Tire Centre has had three previous names. It was originally known as The Palladium, then became the Corel Centre, and was later renamed Scotiabank Place.

The Senators' first game at their new home, known as The Palladium at the time, took place on January 17, 1996. They played the Canadiens and were shut out, 3-0. Despite the Sens' loss during the opening game, support for the team spiked with the new arena opening. The Senators' new home was both fan friendly and state-of-the art, helping the average attendance jump from 10,000 up to 13,000.

The arena has had several name changes over the years, the most recent being in 2013, when it was renamed the Canadian Tire Centre. The arena was upgraded at that time as well, with 700 new high-definition monitors placed throughout the arena, displaying live games from around the NHL, promotions, and contest for fans. In addition to a variety of concessions, the arena also has six restaurants, all open for reservations on game day, as well as a fitness center.

The main events at the Canadian Tire Centre are the 41 Senators' home games, but the arena also hosts basketball games, concerts, and special events. The arena was the site of the 2009 International Ice Hockey Federation (IIHF), the World Junior Championship, the 2013 IIHF Women's World Championship, and a variety of Disney on Ice shows.

One NHL Eastern Conference Championship banner hangs proudly from the rafters of the Senators' arena, reminding fans of their magical run during the 2007 playoffs.

Where They Play

CANADA

British Columbia **7**

Alberta **4**

3

Saskatchewan

Manitoba **14**

Ontario

Washington

Montana

North Dakota

Minnesota **11**

Wisconsin

8

Oregon

Idaho

South Dakota

Iowa

Illinois

Nevada

Utah

Wyoming

Nebraska

6

California

Colorado **9**

Kansas

13 Missouri

5

1

Arizona **2**

New Mexico

Oklahoma

Arkansas

Pacific Ocean

Texas **10**

Louisiana

Missis

UNITED STATES

MEXICO

Gulf of Mexico

NHL WESTERN CONFERENCE ★★★

PACIFIC DIVISION
1 Anaheim Ducks
2 Arizona Coyotes
3 Calgary Flames
4 Edmonton Oilers
5 Los Angeles Kings
6 San Jose Sharks
7 Vancouver Canucks

CENTRAL DIVISION
8 Chicago Blackhawks
9 Colorado Avalanche
10 Dallas Stars
11 Minnesota Wild
12 Nashville Predators
13 St. Louis Blues
14 Winnipeg Jets

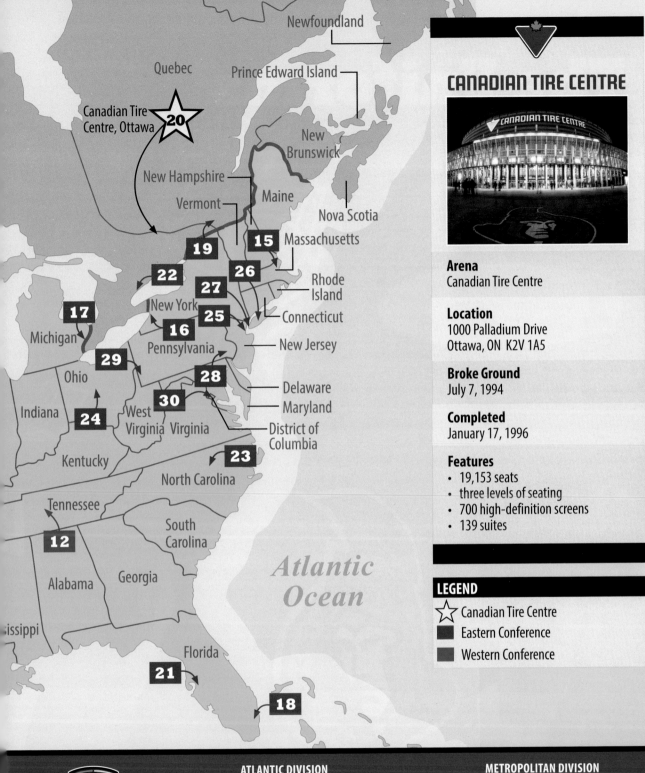

Newfoundland

Quebec

Prince Edward Island

Canadian Tire Centre, Ottawa ⭐ **20**

New Brunswick

New Hampshire

Vermont

Maine

Nova Scotia

19

15 Massachusetts

22

26

27 Rhode Island

New York

25 Connecticut

17

16

Michigan

Pennsylvania

New Jersey

29

Ohio

28

Delaware

Indiana

24

30

West Virginia

Virginia

Maryland

District of Columbia

Kentucky

23

North Carolina

Tennessee

South Carolina

12

Alabama

Georgia

Atlantic Ocean

issippi

Florida

21

18

CANADIAN TIRE CENTRE

Arena
Canadian Tire Centre

Location
1000 Palladium Drive
Ottawa, ON K2V 1A5

Broke Ground
July 7, 1994

Completed
January 17, 1996

Features
- 19,153 seats
- three levels of seating
- 700 high-definition screens
- 139 suites

LEGEND
☆ Canadian Tire Centre
■ Eastern Conference
■ Western Conference

NHL EASTERN CONFERENCE

ATLANTIC DIVISION

15 Boston Bruins	19 Montreal Canadiens
16 Buffalo Sabres	⭐ 20 Ottawa Senators
17 Detroit Red Wings	21 Tampa Bay Lightning
18 Florida Panthers	22 Toronto Maple Leafs

METROPOLITAN DIVISION

23 Carolina Hurricanes	27 New York Rangers
24 Columbus Blue Jackets	28 Philadelphia Flyers
25 New Jersey Devils	29 Pittsburgh Penguins
26 New York Islanders	30 Washington Capitals

The Uniforms

1 Only one jersey number has been retired in Senators history—Frank Finnigan's #8.

The Senators' symbol has always been an image of a Roman general. The team updated the expression on the general's face in 2007, to better represent strength and determination.

Even back in the 1880s, the Senators wore a color scheme consisting of red, black, and white. Over the years, the team has mixed and matched the main colors of its home and away jerseys. The home jerseys changed from primarily white to red, while the away jerseys transformed from mainly black to red before finally landing on the current white background. The **logo** of the Roman general was introduced with the new Senators in 1992, and has varied only slightly since that time.

HOME

AWAY

To date, the team has had four alternate jerseys, and those continue to change. The current alternate jersey has red, white, and black stripes, with a large letter "O" in the center. This jersey looks very similar to the old sweaters worn by the original Senators of the early 1900s.

The team's alternate "heritage" jerseys honor the original Senators, who wore striped sweaters with a large "O" on the front.

Helmets and Face Masks

In April 2013, the Senators wore a **YELLOW RIBBON** decal on their helmets in support of the Canadian Armed Forces.

When Senators players are wearing their alternate uniforms, their helmets do not display the team logo of the Roman general.

The Sens have always had classic white and black helmets to match their jerseys. Their current home helmets are black, and their current away helmets are white. A player's number appears on both the top and back of their helmet, while the team logo appears on each side of the helmet. However, when wearing the alternate striped jerseys, the helmets sport the letter "O" to match the alternate logo.

While position players wear helmets to protect their heads and eyes, goalies wear face masks that offer extra protection from **slap shots** and flailing sticks. Since their face masks are larger than regular hockey helmets, goalies use the mask's blank space as a canvas to display a unique design. Craig Anderson, the Sens' current goalie, has often worn a red, black, white, and gold face mask with the team's logo on it. The team name, "Senators," is written across the bottom of his mask in large white letters.

One of the Senators' first goalies, Daniel Berthiaume, kept his helmet simple— sleek black with the team's logo, and a black face mask to match. Craig Anderson, on the other hand, has created a design with both the Senators' logo and team name featured prominently.

The Coaches

10 The Ottawa Senators have had 10 coaches since they rejoined the NHL in 1992.

Before becoming the head coach of the Senators, Dave Cameron played for the Colorado Rockies and the New Jersey Devils.

The Ottawa Senators have been coached by a variety of well-known figures in the world of hockey. Of the franchise's nine coaches, five were former hockey players, three have won the Jack Adams Award, and one is a member of the Hall of Fame. However, only three of the team's coaches managed to lead the Sens to the playoffs more than once.

JACQUES MARTIN Jacques Martin was the third coach in Senators history. He coached the team for nine years, from 1995 to 2004, the longest period of time any coach has spent behind the bench with the Sens. In those nine years, he led the team to the playoffs eight times. Martin won the Jack Adams Award in 1999 as coach of the year.

BRYAN MURRAY In his three years with the Senators, Bryan Murray successfully took the team to the playoffs three times. The 2006–2007 season marked a high point for the franchise. That year, Murray directed the team to its only Eastern Conference Championship, leading the Senators to their first and only Stanley Cup Final in the modern era.

DAVE CAMERON Former NHL player Dave Cameron assumed the head coaching job in Ottawa after Paul MacLean was replaced 27 games into the 2014–2015 season. Cameron was elevated to the head spot after being an assistant coach for the Senators since 2011. Cameron will be counted on to deliver a playoff berth to Ottawa in his very first season.

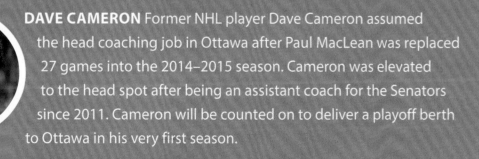

Fans and the Internet

The Senators' fans are extremely dedicated. For the 2013–2014 season, average game attendance was 18,108, and total attendance was 742,468.

The loyal fans of the Ottawa Senators have not allowed the average game attendance to drop below 18,000 since the 2005–2006 season. In recent years, the Sens' average game attendance has been among the highest in the NHL.

During the 2007 playoffs, Senators fans took to the streets to celebrate their team's success, marching down Elgin Street, in a "Sens Mile," before game four of the Eastern Conference Final against the Buffalo Sabres. After winning game five, the street was closed to traffic for a celebration. With such dedicated fans, a network is needed to keep them all connected. On the Senators' website, there is a Fan Zone link, connecting to Facebook, Instagram, and Twitter. There is also a space that displays tweets from Senator players.

Signs
of a fan

#1 Senators fans get into the spirit by dressing up as the team logo, a Roman general.

#2 Fans call themselves members of the "Sens Army," to which fans can also get an official membership. Being a member gives a fan access to discounts, newsletters, contests, and promotions.

Legends of the Past

Many great players have suited up for the Sens. A few of them have become icons of the team and the city it represents.

Jason Spezza

After 10 years with the team, Jason Spezza was named captain for the 2013–2014 season. He was picked by Ottawa during the first round of the 2001 NHL Entry Draft, and is currently ranked second for most goals, **assists**, and points scored on the franchise's all-time list. During his time in Ottawa, Spezza scored 251 goals and dished out 436 assists for a total of 687 points. In 2008 and 2012, Spezza played in the NHL All-Star Game. He was nominated for the Hart Memorial Trophy, as the most valuable player (MVP) of the league, in 2012.

Position: Center
NHL Seasons: 11 (2002–2014)
Born: June 13, 1983, in Mississauga, Ontario, Canada

Position: Right Wing
NHL Seasons: 18 (1995–2014)
Born: December 11, 1972, in Gothenburg, Sweden

Daniel Alfredsson

Daniel Alfredsson was selected by the Senators during the 1994 NHL **Entry Draft**. Throughout his 17 seasons with the team, he played in 1,178 games, a franchise record. Over the years, Alfredsson was nominated several times for various awards. He was an All-Star player for six seasons and won the **Calder Memorial Trophy** in 1996. During his last season with the Senators, in 2012–2013, Alfredsson only played in 47 games but still managed to score 10 goals, two of which were game winners.

Marian Hossa

Marian Hossa was the Senators' first-round pick in the 1997 NHL Entry Draft. He went on to play with the Senators for seven seasons. During that time, he appeared in two All-Star Games. In the Senators' record books, Hossa is ranked fourth with 188 goals, seventh with 202 assists, and sixth with 390 points. Hossa scored a career high of 42 goals with the Sens during the 2002–2003 season. He currently plays for the Chicago Blackhawks.

Position: Right Wing
NHL Seasons: 17 (1997–2014)
Born: January 12, 1979, in Stara Lubovna, Czechoslovakia

Alexei Yashin

Alexei Yashin joined the Senators via the 1992 NHL Entry Draft. Yashin was a first-round choice. While with the Senators, he appeared in the 1994 and 1999 NHL All-Star Games. In his final season with the team, Yashin set a career high with 10 game-winning goals in a season. He was also nominated for the Hart Memorial Trophy and the **Lady Byng Memorial Trophy**. Yashin is ranked third all-time for Senator goals and points. He is also fourth all-time with 273 assists.

Position: Center
NHL Seasons: 12 (1993–2007)
Born: November 5, 1973, in Sverdlovsk, Union of Soviet Socialist Republics

Stars of Today

Today's Senators team is made up of many young, talented players who have proven that they are among the best in the league.

Erik Karlsson

Erik Karlsson was drafted by the Senators in the first round of the 2008 NHL Entry Draft. He was the 15th overall pick. During his five seasons with the team, he was an All-Star three times. In the 2011–2012 season, Karlsson set three career-high marks. He dished out 59 assists, collected 78 total points, and recorded five game-winning goals that season. He was awarded the James Norris Trophy as the NHL's best defenseman for the 2011–2012 season.

Position: Defenseman
NHL Seasons: 5 (2009–Present)
Born: May 31, 1990, in Landsbro, Jonkoping, Sweden

Bobby Ryan

Before joining the Senators, Bobby Ryan played with the Anaheim Ducks, where he tallied career highs of 35 goals in 2009–2010, and 37 assists in 2010–2011. Not only did he score 71 points in 2010–2011, he also had five game-winning goals that year. In the 2008–2009 season, he was nominated for the Calder Memorial Trophy. Ryan was acquired by the Senators via trade in 2013 and completed his first season with the Sens, posting a solid statistical line of 70 games played, 23 goals, and 25 assists.

Position: Left Wing
NHL Seasons: 7 (2007–Present)
Born: March 17, 1987, in Cherry Hill, New Jersey, United States

Craig Anderson

Craig Anderson previously played for the Chicago Blackhawks, the Florida Panthers, and the Colorado Avalanche. On February 18, 2011, he was traded to the Senators. In the season before Anderson was traded, opponents had taken 2,233 shots against him. He set a career high with 2,047 saves that season. That year, Anderson was nominated for the Hart Memorial Trophy and the Vezina Trophy for best goaltender. During the 2012–2013 season, his second with the Sens, Anderson recorded a career-high **save percentage** of 94.1 percent and was once again nominated for both the Hart Memorial Trophy and the Vezina Trophy.

Position: Goaltender
NHL Seasons: 12 (2002–Present)
Born: May 21, 1981, in Park Ridge, Illinois, United States

Kyle Turris

In the 2007 NHL Entry Draft, Kyle Turris was selected as a first-round pick by the Phoenix Coyotes. He played for the Coyotes for four seasons until his trade to Ottawa. Turris notched several career highs during his 2013–2014 season with the Senators, scoring 26 goals, dishing out 32 assists, and scoring five game-winning goals. Turris also has scored two game-winning goals in the playoffs for the Senators, one in 2011–2012 and another in 2012–2013.

Position: Center
NHL Seasons: 7 (2007–Present)
Born: August 14, 1989, in New Westminster, British Columbia, Canada

All-Time Records

1,178
Most Games Played
Daniel Alfredsson has played in 1,178 games as a Senator, more than any other player in franchise history.

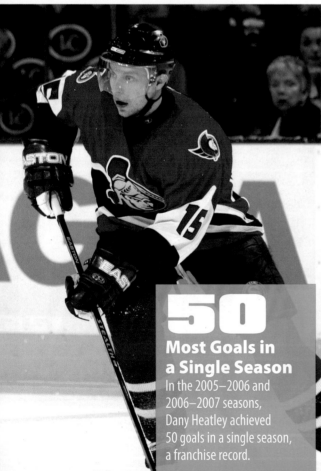

50
Most Goals in a Single Season
In the 2005–2006 and 2006–2007 seasons, Dany Heatley achieved 50 goals in a single season, a franchise record.

71
Most Assists in a Season
During his third season as a Senator, Jason Spezza set a franchise record with 71 assists in one season.

30

Most Shutouts

In his five seasons with the Senators, Patrick Lalime had a total of 30 **shutout** games. Lalime also holds the franchise record for most shutouts in a single season, with eight during the 2002–2003 season.

1,752

Most Saves in a Season

During the 2011–2012 season, Craig Anderson saw 1,917 shots on goal, and saved 1,752 of them.

Timeline

Throughout the team's history, the Senators have had many memorable events that have become defining moments for the team and its fans.

1990
Founders Bruce Firestone, Cyril Leeder, and Randy Sexton are awarded a franchise for Ottawa by the NHL.

1995
The team's first shutout is against the Philadelphia Flyers. The Flyers take 34 shots on goal, but Don Beaupre denies them all.

1988	1990	1992	1994	1996	1998

On October 8, 1992, the Ottawa Senators defeat the Montreal Canadiens, 5–3, in their first game as a franchise at the Ottawa Civic Centre. The team's first goal is made by Neil Brady.

1992
Rick Bowness is named the Senators' first head coach. After four years, he finishes with a coaching record of 39-178-18.

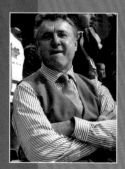

The Future

For more than half of the seasons they have been in existence, the Senators have reached the playoffs, proving to be a smartly run franchise with high-level talent. Although the move to replace coach Paul MacLean early in the 2014-2015 season may seem like a hasty decision upon first glance, it certainly was not. The Senators were able to maintain some continuity by replacing MacLean with assistant coach Dave Cameron. Being a strong defensive team with a promising rookie coach, the Sens may very well have what it takes to take the final step to join the league's elite.

1999

Jacques Martin, the Sens' third coach, wins the Coach of the Year award. He goes on to become the only coach to remain with the team for more than 240 games.

On May 19, 2007, after defeating the Buffalo Sabres, 3–2, in overtime, the Sens advance to the Stanley Cup Final for the first time in franchise history.

2000   2003   2006 ◯   2009   2012   2015

2014

Despite posting a winning record in the 2013–2014 season, the Senators just miss the playoffs, falling five points short of the Detroit Red Wings for the final postseason slot.

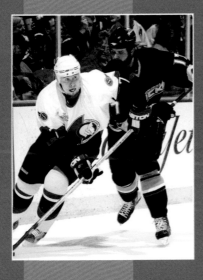

2007

The Senators' run ends as they are eliminated by the Anaheim Ducks in the Stanley Cup Final.

Write a Biography

Life Story

A person's life story can be the subject of a book. This kind of book is called a biography. Biographies often describe the lives of people who have achieved great success. These people may be alive today, or they may have lived many years ago. Reading a biography can help you learn more about a great person.

Get the Facts

Use this book, and research in the library and on the internet, to find out more about your favorite Senator. Learn as much about this player as you can. What position does he play? What are his statistics in important categories? Has he set any records? Also, be sure to write down key events in the person's life. What was his childhood like? What has he accomplished off the field? Is there anything else that makes this person special or unusual?

Use the Concept Web

A concept web is a useful research tool. Read the questions in the concept web on the following page. Answer the questions in your notebook. Your answers will help you write a biography.

Concept Web

Adulthood
- Where does this individual currently reside?
- Does he or she have a family?

Your Opinion
- What did you learn from the books you read in your research?
- Would you suggest these books to others?
- Was anything missing from these books?

Accomplishments off the Field
- What is this person's life's work?
- Has he or she received awards or recognition for accomplishments?
- How have this person's accomplishments served others?

Write a Biography

Childhood
- Where and when was this person born?
- Describe his or her parents, siblings, and friends.
- Did this person grow up in unusual circumstances?

Help and Obstacles
- Did this individual have a positive attitude?
- Did he or she receive help from others?
- Did this person have a mentor?
- Did this person face any hardships?
- If so, how were the hardships overcome?

Accomplishments on the Field
- What records does this person hold?
- What key games and plays have defined his career?
- What are his stats in categories important to his position?

Work and Preparation
- What was this person's education?
- What was his or her work experience?
- How does this person work?
- What is the process he or she uses?

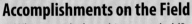

Trivia Time

Take this quiz to test your knowledge of the Senators. The answers are printed upside down under each question.

1 What is the current name of the team's arena?

A. Canadian Tire Centre

2 Who is the current coach of the Senators?

A. Dave Cameron

3 What do Ottawa fans dress up as for games?

A. Roman generals

4 What is the Senators' alternate logo?

A. The letter "O"

5 How many Stanley Cups have the Senators won?

A. Zero

6 Who played in the most games as a Senator?

A. Daniel Alfredsson

7 Which NHL coach led the Senators to their first Stanley Cup Final?

A. Bryan Murray

8 How many times have the Senators appeared in the Stanley Cup Final?

A. One

9 What is the Ottawa Senators' nickname?

A. The Sens

Key Words

All-Star: a game made for the best-ranked players in the NHL that happens mid-season. A player can be named an All-Star and then be sent to play in this game.

assists: a statistic that is attributed to up to two players of the scoring team who shoot, pass, or deflect the puck toward the scoring teammate

Calder Memorial Trophy: an award given out annually to the hockey player who is considered "the most proficient in his first year of competition" in the NHL

entry draft: an annual meeting where different teams in the NHL are allowed to pick new, young players who can join their teams

franchise: a team that is a member of a professional sports league

Lady Byng Memorial Trophy: a trophy given to a player in the NHL who exhibits great playing skills as well as great conduct off the ice

logo: a symbol that stands for a team or organization

playoffs: a series of games that occur after regular season play

save percentage: the rate at which a goalie stops shots being made toward his net by the opposing team

shutout: a game in which the losing team is blocked from making any goals

slap shots: hard shots made by raising the stick about waist high before striking the puck with a sharp slapping motion

Index

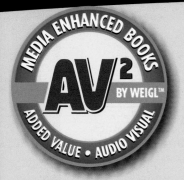

Log on to www.av2books.com

AV² by Weigl brings you media enhanced books that support active learning. Go to www.av2books.com, and enter the special code found on page 2 of this book. You will gain access to enriched and enhanced content that supplements and complements this book. Content includes video, audio, weblinks, quizzes, a slide show, and activities.

AV² Online Navigation

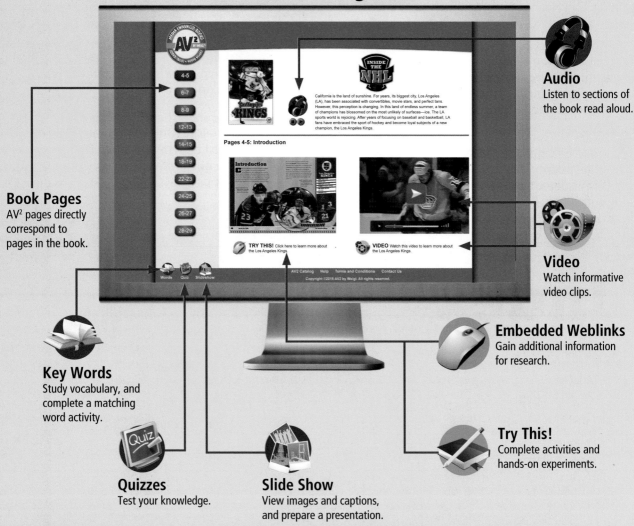

Book Pages
AV² pages directly correspond to pages in the book.

Audio
Listen to sections of the book read aloud.

Video
Watch informative video clips.

Key Words
Study vocabulary, and complete a matching word activity.

Embedded Weblinks
Gain additional information for research.

Quizzes
Test your knowledge.

Slide Show
View images and captions, and prepare a presentation.

Try This!
Complete activities and hands-on experiments.

AV² was built to bridge the gap between print and digital. We encourage you to tell us what you like and what you want to see in the future.

Sign up to be an AV² Ambassador at www.av2books.com/ambassador.